T0030167

What Do We Know About the Winchester House?

by Emma Carlson Berne

illustrated by Ted Hammond

Penguin Workshop

For Sara, my sister—ECB

To my mom—TH

PENGUIN WORKSHOP
An imprint of Penguin Random House LLC, New York

First published in the United States of America by Penguin Workshop,
an imprint of Penguin Random House LLC, New York, 2023

Copyright © 2023 by Penguin Random House LLC

Penguin supports copyright. Copyright fuels creativity, encourages diverse voices,
promotes free speech, and creates a vibrant culture. Thank you for buying an authorized
edition of this book and for complying with copyright laws by not reproducing, scanning,
or distributing any part of it in any form without permission. You are supporting writers
and allowing Penguin to continue to publish books for every reader.

PENGUIN is a registered trademark and PENGUIN WORKSHOP is a trademark
of Penguin Books Ltd. WHO HQ & Design is a registered trademark
of Penguin Random House LLC.

Visit us online at penguinrandomhouse.com.

Library of Congress Cataloging-in-Publication Data is available.

Printed in the United States of America

ISBN 9780593519295 (paperback)   10 9 8 7 6 5 4 3 2 1 WOR
ISBN 9780593519301 (library binding)   10 9 8 7 6 5 4 3 2 1 WOR

The publisher does not have any control over and does not assume any responsibility
for author or third-party websites or their content.

Contents

What Do We Know About the Winchester House?

In the spring of 1886, a well-dressed woman rolled into the Santa Clara Valley, California, in her carriage. Her name was Sarah Winchester. She was a widow, and she was very rich. She had moved from New Haven, Connecticut, on the East Coast, and she wanted warm weather, peace and quiet, and lots of space.

Sarah, who was nearly fifty years old, moved into an eight-room farmhouse on forty-five acres that she called Llanada (ya-NAH-dah) Villa— Spanish for "the house on the plain." Almost right away, she began building. In the first six months after she moved in, the house grew to twenty-six rooms!

The ambitious woman never really stopped

building. Over the next thirty-six years, Llanada Villa, later known as Winchester House, grew from eight rooms to a hundred and sixty rooms. Spreading over six acres, the size of more than six football fields, the enormous house eventually

had six kitchens, two thousand doors, thirteen bathrooms, forty-seven staircases, and ten thousand windows!

No plans were drawn, and no architects had been hired. Sarah ordered her builders to add

rooms wherever she wanted them, and if she didn't like how the room looked, she would order them to tear it down. Then she would ask them to start over.

Sarah loved her house. She decorated it with expensive wood floors and paneling made of rare teak, mahogany, and rosewood. The sunlight streamed through elaborate stained glass windows. Flowered tiles surrounded the fireplaces, and very expensive wallpaper covered the walls. Llanada Villa was a beautiful home.

Llanada Villa is now called Winchester House. And it is still quite beautiful. But visitors to the home today find that it is also very odd. One stairway goes up seven steps. Then it goes down eleven. One doorway opens out into midair. Take an extra step, and you'll plummet into a kitchen eight feet below! The rooms and hallways twist and turn like a maze. Anyone could get lost.

Why did Sarah build her house so strangely? Why are there so many things numbering thirteen in the house—thirteen bathrooms, thirteen holes in a sink drain, and thirteen windows in the thirteenth bathroom? And thirteen gas jets on the grand chandelier in the ballroom!

Why are there so many hidden passageways and odd openings to look through?

Llanada Villa started as a simple farmhouse. Sarah Winchester built it into a massive, confusing mansion. Over time, stories grew and grew about *why* her house looked the way it did. Was the house haunted by spirits? Did Sarah Winchester invite those spirits into her home? Today, people are still asking those questions. Visitors can take tours and wander the bewildering rooms that Sarah Winchester built at Llanada Villa. Will they meet spirits and ghosts as well? Some say they have. Others say the mysterious house is simply misunderstood and perhaps not quite haunted. But no one can know for sure.

CHAPTER 1
Life in New Haven

Sarah Pardee Winchester was not the first Sarah in her family. She was the third. Her mother was named Sarah. And eight years before Sarah Winchester's birth in 1839, a different Sarah had been born. She was the first child of Leonard and Sarah Pardee. This little Sarah died when she was only eighteen months old.

The Pardees had two more daughters, Mary and Nettie, and a son named Leonard after his father. By the time their third daughter was born, they were ready for another Sarah.

Sarah was born in a pretty, tree-filled neighborhood of New Haven, Connecticut, where her family had lived for generations. They were kind, educated people. Sarah's father was a carpenter. Her mother took care of the house and the children. But when a fire in 1837 destroyed part of the city, Leonard's carpentry business was destroyed as well. Some people in New Haven had lost everything, so they did not have money to pay a carpenter, even though there was plenty of rebuilding to be done. Instead, Leonard took a job watching over the public baths—a place where people who didn't have private bathrooms could wash—in New Haven. The family lived in their own rooms there, like a private apartment.

A few years after the fire, Leonard started working as a carpenter again. When Sarah was around seven or eight, Leonard set up a full-time carpenter's shop. Sarah grew up surrounded by planks and pieces of wood, paint, axes, planes, and saws. She watched her father and his helpers craft pedals for pianos, hitching posts for horses, doors, and window frames. Her interest in building and woodworking grew. Later, she would put all this knowledge to use when building her own home.

By the early 1850s, when Sarah was a young teenager, the family was starting to recover from their setbacks due to the New Haven fire.

Leonard made good money as a carpenter, and the Pardees moved to a big house in a nice neighborhood. Leonard expanded his carpentry shop, and the family grew wealthier. The Pardees were now well-known and respected in New Haven. Sarah was taught by a private French tutor and took music lessons. She dressed in fancy clothes. She was shy but lively.

But Sarah wouldn't stay home forever. At the time, women were expected to get married and move out of their parents' homes. When she was in her early twenties, Sarah began dating William Winchester. She'd known him for many years—the Pardees and the Winchesters had been next-door neighbors. Their families went to the same church, and Sarah's father helped fix the machines at William's father's shirt factory. Sarah had grown up with William. Now he was getting ready to work for his father at his family's huge shirt factory and mill. William would one day be a rich man.

William Winchester

At this time, the United States was edging closer and closer to civil war. And on April 12, 1861, Confederate soldiers attacked Fort Sumter in South Carolina. When war broke out, Sarah's brother was one of the first to volunteer to fight. He left New Haven on April 21, 1861, and he joined the Second Connecticut Infantry. About a year later, Sarah and William married in a quiet ceremony.

The United States Civil War

Between 1861 and 1865, Southern states and Northern states fought in a bloody civil war in which over seven hundred thousand soldiers died. At the heart of the war was the issue of slavery. Many people considered the enslavement of others to be wrong. But Southern states depended on enslaved Black people to plant and harvest crops like cotton and rice that kept white landowners wealthy. Northern states had more factories and industries in addition to agriculture. They were less dependent on slavery to keep their economy going. The argument over the need for slavery created a huge divide among the American people. Eleven Southern states withdrew from the United States and formed their own Confederate States of America. The Confederate soldiers fought the Northern Union soldiers.

On April 9, 1865, the Confederates surrendered.
The Union had won the war. The Southern states were
brought back into the Union, and on December 18,
1865, slavery was ended in the United States.

Sarah's brother fought in the First Battle of Bull Run in Manassas, Virginia, one of the first major battles of the war. Under the hot July sun, the Union troops fought fiercely but, in the end, could not defeat the Confederates there.

First Battle of Bull Run

He returned home after Bull Run. He had been in the army for three months. His family breathed a sigh of relief that he was safe. Sarah's sister's husband, Homer, fought for four years in the Union Army and also came home safely.

As the war drew to a close, life seemed good for Sarah and her family. Their loved ones had survived the fighting. Sarah and William had a lovely home with his parents and plenty of money. The Union had won the war. The Winchesters must have surely believed the worst times were now behind them. But they were wrong.

CHAPTER 2
Tragedy Strikes

William Winchester's family was very wealthy. Their shirt factory, the Winchester & Davies Shirt Manufactory, was successful. But before the Civil War, William's father, Oliver, had also invested money in another company, one that manufactured guns. The Volcanic Repeating Arms Company made a type of gun called the "Winchester repeater," and it was very popular.

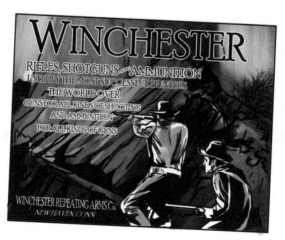

The Winchester Repeater

Before the founders of the Volcanic Repeating Arms Company invented a gun that could fire multiple bullets one after the other, guns could only fire one bullet at a time. Then the person shooting had to stop and reload the gun.

Oliver Winchester thought that this type of gun, called a repeater, could become very popular. He had one of the mechanics from his shirt factory design a specific type of repeating gun that was a rifle. This gun came to be called the Winchester repeater, and over the years, the company's name became the Winchester Repeating Arms Company.

Winchester rifles were popular internationally. They were sold to armies in Europe and Asia. But they were even more popular in the United States, where white settlers used them against Native Americans, tribal nations acquired them to fight back, and ranchers and cowboys used them for hunting. The gun was both a useful tool and a deadly weapon.

It made the Winchester family lots of money. Sarah would be wealthy for the rest of her life.

In 1865, Sarah learned that she was pregnant. Everyone was excited, especially William. He and Sarah couldn't wait to be parents.

Baby Annie was born on June 15, 1866, when Sarah was twenty-seven years old. Sarah had her daughter at home, like most women at that time. She was a healthy baby, and her parents adored her.

But as the days went by, Sarah and William realized that something was wrong with the baby. She wasn't eating. She couldn't seem to digest her milk, and she was losing weight, fast. Sarah was frantic. She had waited three years for a child, and now her daughter seemed to be fading in front of her eyes. They called in a special nurse to feed Annie. A doctor came.

But he couldn't do anything for the sick baby.
Annie cried and cried, night and day. She was
starving to death, and the doctor said the baby
had a disease that might be keeping her from
digesting food.

Baby Annie died at only five weeks old, on July 25. Her tiny body was buried at the family cemetery. William and Sarah would never have another child.

Sarah and William tried to recover from the death of their baby by working on their plans for a huge mansion they were building in New Haven that they would share with William's parents. This giant house would have marble floors, chandeliers, and floor-to-ceiling windows. Both William and Sarah threw themselves into the work of going over the architect's plans, supervising the workmen, and choosing the stone, wood, and wallpaper for the rooms inside. Sarah loved it all.

Building construction and designing houses were
her passions, and they were good distractions

from her heartbreak. They moved into the house in 1868.

William and Sarah were happy in their
new house. They loved it, and they loved each
other. William worked as the secretary for the
family gun company. Sometimes, William and

Sarah went with William's father, Oliver, on business trips. They most likely had friends and family over to their house for dinners and parties.

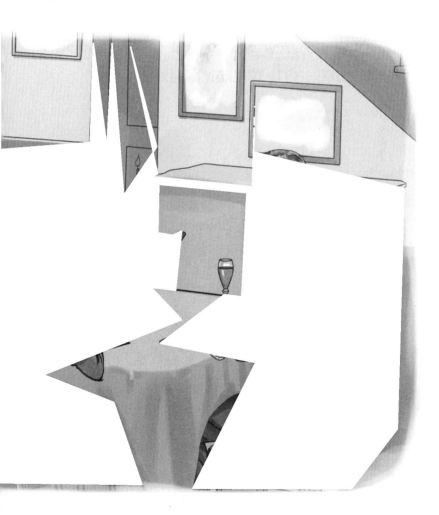

But William was sick. For a long time, he had been weak and coughing. The cold, snowy winters of the Northeast made him cough even more. He had tuberculosis, a disease caused by bacteria that infect a person's lungs. There was no cure. William grew weaker and weaker. Finally, on March 7, 1881, William died.

Sarah was overcome with grief. She dressed in black and draped a heavy black lace veil over her head. She was only a little more than forty years old, but she would never remarry, and she would never forget William.

Sarah Winchester

Sarah wanted a fresh start. New Haven was too full of sad memories. And Sarah already had arthritis in her hands and other joints. The cold of Connecticut made the aching worse. She had inherited William's part of the Winchester Repeating Arms Company, and now she was one of the richest women in New England. She had enough money to move wherever she chose to.

Sarah traveled to the beach to rest, and then she went to Europe. But she wasn't happy coming and going. She was also no longer content with her home in New Haven. She wanted something completely different. She wanted a life that was all her own, away from the Winchester family.

Sarah and William had once traveled to California on business for the Winchester rifle company. She liked the sunshine and the warm, clear weather. Sarah made up her mind. In 1885, she packed up and set out for the Santa Clara Valley. She was going to find a piece of land and do what she loved best: build a house.

CHAPTER 3
Going to California

In the 1880s, the Santa Clara Valley was full of fruit farms and wheat farms. But Santa Clara was changing fast. Sarah Winchester wasn't the

only person who had heard of the beauty of California. The area was booming. In huge numbers, all kinds of people were moving to the valley from the East Coast. When Sarah arrived in the mid-1880s, several wealthy families already lived on large, luxurious ranches in the area.

Sarah's friend, Ned Rambo, showed her around the farmland in the valley. Golden hills were covered in sunshine and orchards, and fields of crops lined the quiet roads. The valley was only thirty miles from the bustle of San Francisco. Sarah loved the area. She told Ned she wanted to buy a farm.

He knew just the right place. There was a piece of property for sale near his own house, he told Sarah. When they drove out, Sarah saw a quiet forty-five-acre spot that had been part of a wheat farm and then a fruit farm. The views of the hills were gorgeous. The farm had a house, but it was only eight rooms and very plain. Surely, that wouldn't work for Sarah, Ned thought. She was used to all kinds of luxury.

Original farmhouse

But the house didn't bother Sarah at all. She loved architecture, construction, and building. She had plenty of money for improvements. This building would become a project for her.

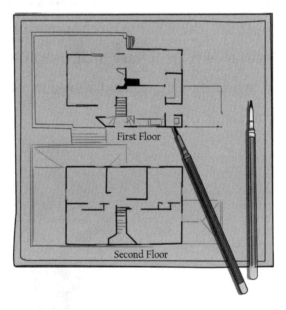

First Floor

Second Floor

To an outsider, Sarah seemed like she would fit in just fine. She was a rich heiress—a woman who had inherited property and wealth—and she was going to build a mansion where an eight-room farmhouse had once stood.

But Sarah did not fit in with the rest of the families in the area. Right from the start, she declared that she would not be hiring an architect to design her mansion. She would be her own architect. She was going to lead the building process, too, and be her own foreman and contractor.

This was highly unusual, whispered the wealthy society families of the area. It was very odd for women to be architects or contractors. They wondered: What is Sarah Winchester doing? Sarah paid no attention to the gossip. She moved in with her niece Daisy Merriman and her servants. Wagons full of expensive lumber, loads of

Marion Isabel "Daisy" Merriman

brick and stone, and carefully wrapped bundles of stained glass began to arrive at the house. The deliveries would roll down the road to the house and disappear from view. Sarah planted a thick, high hedge between her house and the road. She wanted total privacy.

Behind the hedge, Sarah gave orders to her workers. Unlike trained architects who draw and design an entire building at once, Sarah planned only a few rooms at a time, tacking them on wherever she wanted. If she didn't like the rooms once they were finished, she'd order her builders to tear them down and start over. Sometimes, she would tell them to stop working on a section of the house she'd lost interest in. Leaving that part unfinished, Sarah would order them to begin work on a different wing.

The construction and the pounding never stopped. The neighbors said to one another that it seemed as if the noise went on all day and all night, all week long. The house grew and grew. Workers built a third story. Then a fourth story. Sarah ordered a seven-story tower to be built. She told the workers to redo the top part sixteen times! Gorgeous rolls of expensive wallpaper were delivered. Workers fitted beautiful stained glass into specially built windows.

Sarah installed indoor plumbing and even an early form of electricity.

As the house grew, Sarah retreated. She almost never went out. When she did, she wrapped herself in a thick black veil. She allowed no one into the house except servants; her niece and companion, Daisy; and the workmen who carried out her orders. She didn't have tea parties or invite neighbors to visit. Even Sarah's letters home to New Haven implied that she didn't have room for guests and that it would be better if her family did not visit her. Sarah wanted to be alone. She never explained why.

Sarah could not even be bothered to host a president. In 1901, US president William McKinley visited nearby San Jose. It seemed as if Sarah would be the best choice to invite him for a visit. After all, she was the richest woman in the area; she had a huge, luxurious home; and her name was recognized as the brand of a famous American gun company. President McKinley had even known her husband, William. Although her neighbors expected her to extend an invitation, Sarah did not ask President McKinley to her home. Instead, the sixty-two-year-old widow stayed silent inside Llanada Villa.

President William McKinley

But Llanada Villa wasn't Sarah's only home. Around 1903, Sarah's niece Daisy was married. She wanted a life that included more than being a companion to her aunt. Sarah bought a house in a nearby neighborhood called Atherton, to be closer to Daisy and her husband. Sarah also bought other houses in Atherton. She gave one to Daisy and her husband, even though they had their own home. She lived in another part-time and at Llanada Villa part-time. Daisy continued to work for her aunt as her companion, even after her marriage.

Sarah Winchester's Atherton home

Gossip about Sarah continued to grow, just as the house called Llanada Villa did. Why would she build such a large house and not share it or show it to anyone? Didn't she want to have parties and balls in the grand ballroom? Why did she always wear a veil? What was she hiding? And why was her house so strange looking?

CHAPTER 4
The Earth Moves

At 5:12 in the morning on April 18, 1906, most people in Northern California were asleep in their beds. Sarah Winchester, now sixty-seven, was asleep as well. Then, the earth shook violently. From San Francisco to Santa Clara to what is now Salinas, a huge earthquake toppled buildings in an instant. Streets buckled and snapped. Bridges collapsed. Fires burned through the city.

Llanada Villa was a wreck. The seven-story tower had collapsed in a heap, showering rocks and glass into the garden and lower rooms.

Two upper additions crumbled, and all the chimneys fell in. Sarah's home had been her haven. She'd never stopped working on it. She had chosen every slab of wood and every tile with care. Now, so much of it was ruined.

As Californians recovered from the earthquake, they also rebuilt their houses. They wanted to show the world and one another that nothing, not even a massive earthquake, could keep them down.

The San Francisco Earthquake

The almost 8.0 earthquake that shook California on April 18, 1906, toppled buildings as if they were made of glass. Scientists today estimate that the shaking stretched almost three hundred miles along the California coast. Collapsed buildings killed over three thousand people. Survivors remembered furniture sliding across rooms and huge chunks of stone falling from buildings onto people below. One man remembered his bed bucking up and down as if he were riding a horse.

Sacramento

San Francisco

Epicenter

San Jose

Los Angeles

California

The earthquake lasted less than a minute. But the devastation was near total. And when it was over, the San Francisco City Hall stood with only its dome intact. The collapsed walls all around looked as if they had been shredded.

But even more destructive than the violent movement of the earth was the fire that broke out in San Francisco as a result of the earthquake. It burned for four days over five square miles of the city and destroyed close to twenty-eight thousand homes and businesses. Over half of the entire population of San Francisco was left homeless, sleeping in the streets and in tents in parks.

But Sarah didn't rebuild. She cleared away the rubble, and then she ordered a new roof built, right on top of the half-destroyed house. That was all the major rebuilding she was willing to do. She never made any more large additions to Llanada Villa, which now looked stranger than ever. She lived at times at her various other homes in the neighborhood of Atherton.

Because Sarah didn't act like most other rich people, rumors about her spread. The local newspapers invented stories about what was going on in that unusual house. One rumor was that Sarah practiced the art of spiritualism— talking to the spirits of the dead. People wondered if perhaps she spoke to her dead husband and daughter. They said she communicated alone with the spirits in a special room called the séance (say: SAY-ahns) room. (A séance is a meeting where people attempt to make contact with the dead.) It was rumored that she wore one of thirteen different-colored robes that hung on thirteen hooks, and that she was obsessed with the supernatural and the number thirteen.

Fed by rumors, people began to believe that the house was haunted with the ghosts of the people killed by the guns manufactured by her husband's company. They thought that Sarah talked with them during eerie, late-night meetings. One person thought that the spirits had sent her a warning before the earthquake. They told her she had spent too much money on the house. When the front rooms were destroyed in the earthquake, they believed that Sarah had obeyed the spirits and forever closed off thirty front rooms.

As the local rumors went on, Sarah was not at peace. In fact, people whispered that she was terrified of the supposed ghosts that lived in her house.

People claimed she never slept in the same bedroom two nights in a row, in order to confuse the spirits that she believed were following her. Neighbors said they heard mysterious bells chiming at midnight and at two o'clock in the morning. Were the  sounds meant to summon spirits? Or to keep them away? Sensational stories about the house grew as they were told and retold. These stories described the house as something from a dream, with so many windows and doors and odd twists and turns, that people felt as if the house were shifting around them.

What Is Spiritualism?

If Sarah Winchester was a spiritualist, she wasn't alone. The practice of communicating with the spirits of the dead through a person called a medium was very popular near the end of the nineteenth century and into the twentieth.

Spiritualists believed that the spirits of the dead could offer them advice or even answer questions. To contact spirits, they would hold a gathering called a séance. They would pay a medium to lead the gathering for them. Sitting in a circle and often holding hands, the group would wait for the medium to contact someone who had died. Then, the medium would ask the spirits questions. The spirits might answer by making noises in the room or by moving furniture. The medium might hold a pen and allow the spirits to guide their hand in writing an answer on paper.

No one can know for sure if the events that happen at a séance are real. But the thought that one could communicate with the people they loved who were no longer with them was a great comfort to those who practiced spiritualism, as well as a profitable career for mediums.

But these were rumors. Sarah's servants and companions never confirmed them. No one can say for certain if Sarah did hold these solo séances. If Sarah was a spiritualist, she kept that to herself. She never spoke out to say that the rumors and newspaper stories were lies. She never spoke about it at all. As she grew older,

she left the house less and less. She never gave interviews. She let the thick hedges grow up around her property so it was totally cut off from view. On the rare occasions that she did go out, she kept herself wrapped in her thick veil, so no one could see her face, and she stayed in her carriage.

The years went by. When her beloved niece Daisy became sick from appendicitis, Sarah realized she needed more help than Daisy could provide. Daisy retired from her official job as Sarah's companion, though she probably still helped out from time to time. Soon, Sarah hired a new helper, Henrietta Sivera. Henrietta made appointments for Sarah, answered the phone for her, and kept her company, just as Daisy had done.

Henrietta Sivera

Although no more major additions to the house were built in the years after the earthquake, Sarah kept minor building projects going. The hammering went on.

Newspapers published interviews with people who said that Sarah Winchester believed that if the building ever stopped, she would die. These stories were not based on facts or on quotes from Sarah herself. But the rumors continued and became stranger. Some people came to believe that Sarah was determined to keep building, even if it was just hammering in a nail, until the moment of her death.

CHAPTER 5
From Llanada Villa to Winchester House

As Sarah Winchester grew older, her arthritis became worse. Whichever of her houses she was staying in, she lived with only her paid companion, Henrietta, and servants. She seemed  to prefer it that way. It was how she had lived for decades. On September 5, 1922, Sarah died of heart failure. She was eighty-three years old.

Sarah had a small funeral that she had planned herself. She had written out a careful will that left money to her nieces and nephews, her longtime servants, her current and former companions Henrietta and Daisy, and to a few charities in San Jose. Her other houses and stocks were to be sold and the money divided. But when the appraiser—a person whose job it is to assess the value of the house—came to look at Llanada Villa, he saw the strange structure and the odd roof that had been rebuilt after the earthquake.

Even though the house was filled with expensive wood, marble, and stained glass, he shook his head. "No value," he wrote. He felt that the masterpiece of Sarah Winchester's life was worth almost nothing. The land was valued more highly than the house.

The developer in charge of the property divided up the grounds. One piece of land included the house. The other did not. The land sold quickly.

The house did not. No one wanted Llanada Villa, the house that had been so oddly constructed.

Or so it seemed. John Brown was a businessman who owned amusement parks and carnival rides. And he knew that other "mysterious" houses were able to earn lots of money for their owners. Tour guides would spin tales of ghosts and hauntings while walking groups of tourists through the rooms. Llanada Villa, John thought, could be the next "mystery house."

John bought the house, and by spring 1923, less than a year after Sarah's death, San Jose's newest haunted house was open for business. Llanada Villa had a new name. It was now called "the Winchester House."

Eager for paying visitors, John invited local journalists to tour the house while he told them juicy details of ghosts, spirits, and a strange woman who spoke to them from inside the mansion's walls.

The reporters loved the creepy house and published articles about how very odd the Winchester House was.

When the well-known escape artist Harry Houdini visited California in 1924, John Brown invited him to spend the night inside Winchester House. Houdini declared that he would investigate the reports of ghosts and spirits and see if they were true. And John would get some great publicity for his newest attraction.

At the time, Houdini was one of the most famous people in the world. He said he would tour the house at midnight.

John Brown was probably thrilled when Houdini described the house as "a marvelous place." The house's reputation as a haunted place grew, and tourists lined up to see for themselves. John and the other managers of the Winchester House repeated over and over the stories of ghosts and spirits and odd Mrs. Winchester.

Harry Houdini (1874–1926)

Erich Weisz was born in Budapest, Hungary, in 1874. He began performing onstage when he was twenty years old, first as a magician and then as an escape artist. He used the stage name Harry Houdini and specialized in escaping from locked chains and shackles. He could also pick locks, escape from jail cells, free himself from straitjackets, and hold his breath underwater for more than three minutes. His act often seemed to put his life at risk, which thrilled the audiences who came to see him.

Houdini was also interested in proving whether spiritualists, mediums, and others who claimed to communicate with the dead were lying or not. He would investigate their claims and then declare his findings to the public, often exposing them as fakes. He always promised his wife, Bess, that if he died before her, he would try to figure out a way to send her a message.

The great escape artist who could survive being submerged upside down in water while locked in a straitjacket died from a simple cause: a ruptured appendix, when he was only fifty-two. Although Bess held séances once a year for ten years, waiting for a message from Harry, she finally gave up. Harry was truly gone.

Other people wanted some of the Winchester attention, too. Sarah's neighbor Edith Daley published a series of newspaper articles in

Edith Daley

1922, describing her thoughts about the strange house. She repeated the rumor that Sarah believed she would die if the construction ever stopped. At the moment of her death, Edith said, all the hammering and sawing from the house suddenly went silent.

Edith also reported that Sarah once ordered the wine cellar double-locked, *forever*, after she found a black handprint just outside it. She thought that the handprint was left by someone who had planted a bomb in there. It was Edith's opinion that Sarah spent her days haunted by the memories of those killed by her husband's family's Winchester rifles.

No one had any way of confirming what Edith and others wrote. But they didn't much care if they were reading fact or fiction. Newspapers at the time often published rumors and gossip without checking to see if what they were printing was true.

But what *was* the truth?

CHAPTER 6
The Other Sarah Winchester

What if Sarah was not obsessed with spirits or her long-dead daughter and husband? What if the house wasn't haunted with anything but sawdust and the smell of fresh paint? What if Sarah was nothing more than a caring person who was in a lot of pain and preferred to be alone?

Her house was odd, that was for sure. And Sarah lived her life in an unusual way. She didn't do the things that wealthy women in small towns were supposed to do. People noticed. Newspaper reporters noticed. And they made up stories about why Sarah did the things she did: ghosts, spirits, and strange obsessions. The reality may have been quite different.

Sarah truly loved construction and architecture, ever since her early days watching her father build and work with wood. When she moved to Llanada Villa, she decided that she was going to do what *she* enjoyed. She was going to build any kind of house she felt like, and she was going to be in charge of it. In Sarah's day, women were not building contractors or architects. They left those jobs to men. But Sarah didn't care. Because she was so independent, people decided she was strange. And Sarah most likely wasn't very odd at all. In fact, even though she lived far from her family, she was very close to her servants,

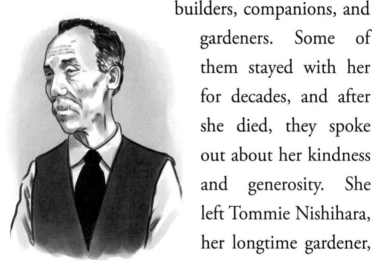

Tommie Nishihara

builders, companions, and gardeners. Some of them stayed with her for decades, and after she died, they spoke out about her kindness and generosity. She left Tommie Nishihara, her longtime gardener, money in her will. She donated over $2 million to create a hospital in New Haven in honor of her husband: the William Wirt Winchester Hospital.

William Wirt Winchester Hospital

When her family members asked for money, she gave it to them. She didn't want to visit with them, but she wasn't selfish. She just liked to be alone.

Many have said that the rumors about the nonstop building at Llanada Villa were simply made up. There was a lot of hammering and sawing, which may have seemed nonstop to the neighbors. But building *did* stop for long stretches over the years while Sarah decided what to build next or waited for deliveries.

And Sarah had good reasons for staying in her house. She had painful arthritis, which had affected her since she was a young woman. Walking hurt. Her hands and feet were stiff and perhaps misshapen. In addition to that, Sarah had lost many of her teeth. She felt embarrassed about how she looked.

So, when she went out, Sarah preferred to wrap her face in a heavy black veil. She didn't get out of her carriage because her joints hurt so much. She wasn't so mysterious. She was just an old woman, and she had a disease. The stories of who Sarah was and what her house looked like are forever linked. But now it's possible to see that even the strange and creepy parts of the house itself made sense, especially when seen as a result of the 1906 earthquake.

The doors that open onto sheer drop-offs? The hallways and rooms that would have extended out were destroyed in the earthquake. Sarah simply never sealed off the doors. The staircase that ends at the ceiling? There were once several stories above it, until the earthquake sheared them off. Sarah put on a roof, but she never removed the staircase. Chimneys that broke off halfway were simply closed over but left as they were.

Sarah wrote to her relatives that she felt terrible about the destruction to her home. And lots of other people in California felt the same way about their own houses, barns, factories, and businesses. But after the earthquake, people decided that the proper thing to do was to rebuild and not let themselves be defeated.

All over the area the earthquake had damaged, people wanted to erase the memories of this awful event. They wanted to rebuild so that you couldn't even tell there had been an earthquake.

But Sarah was heartbroken at the ruin of her beautiful home. And she refused to rebuild.

CHAPTER 7
Rumors Take Over

For most of Sarah Winchester's life, women could not vote. Most married women, especially wealthy ones, did not have jobs. Heiresses like Sarah were supposed to host parties and charity events and to visit with one another for tea or lunch.

After William died, Sarah refused to have parties, host galas, and visit with other ladies. She worked hard, putting in long hours building a house, which no other ladies did. She refused to host President William McKinley or to rebuild after the earthquake. When rumors started spreading about her, Sarah never spoke out against them. She did what she wanted, the way she wanted.

Hers was a strange lifestyle. And Sarah became an easy target for rumors and wild stories.

Journalists in San Jose and the Santa Clara Valley knew that juicy stories about the mysterious widow with the weird house would sell lots of newspapers. So they wrote a lot of articles.

In particular, they focused on the Winchester family business, the Winchester Repeating Arms Company.

In the early 1920s, the country was thinking about the horrors of World War I and the violence that guns could cause. Many people all over the country were writing about a new idea: that guns weren't just a necessary way to survive but that they could be very, very harmful in the wrong hands. People began feeling bad about the tens of thousands of victims who had been shot by guns in the history of the United States.

When John Brown bought Llanada Villa after Sarah's death, he used both Sarah's house and her life story for entertainment. Sarah was obsessed with the number thirteen, John's tour guides told their visitors. They would name all the thirteens in the house: the number

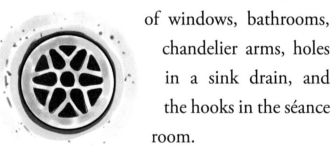

of windows, bathrooms, chandelier arms, holes in a sink drain, and the hooks in the séance room.

Sink drain

But Sarah's carpenter James Perkins, who worked in the house for many years, spoke up. He said that some of these "thirteens" were added by John's company, after Sarah's death, to create the story that she was fascinated by the world of spirits and ghosts. For example, the thirteenth chandelier arm does not match the others because it was added after John Brown bought the house.

Unlucky Thirteen?

Sarah Winchester's obsession with the number thirteen might have been only a made-up story to entertain visitors. But if it was true, she would have a lot of company. The number thirteen is

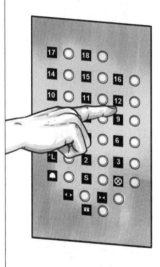

widely considered unlucky in Europe and the United States. Some hotels don't have a thirteenth floor. The buttons on most elevator panels go from twelve to fourteen. At some airports, the gate numbers also skip the number thirteen.

No one knows exactly how thirteen came to be viewed as such an unlucky number, but historians believe it may have to do with the story of Jesus and the Last Supper. Jesus invited followers to join him at what became the last supper before his death, the story goes. The last and thirteenth person to arrive was Judas, who betrayed Jesus and caused his death.

A different and even older story of how thirteen came to be so unlucky is from Norse mythology. According to legend, the god Loki stormed into a dinner party attended by twelve other gods. He was the thirteenth guest, and his appearance threw the whole party into chaos (disorder and confusion). After Loki shot Balder, the god of joy, the whole world, like the party of the gods, was thrown into chaos.

Sarah's companion, Henrietta, also read the stories John Brown was telling about Winchester House. She was furious. She called Brown a liar and said that he was not telling the truth about what life was like behind the doors of Llanada Villa. The hooks and the colored robes in the séance room were never there when Sarah was alive.

John Brown

And how could she even have had séances in that room? Séances are held with a group of people, and of course, Sarah never had visitors. The house was odd. It was strange. No one could argue with that. But it wasn't haunted. Even though Henrietta insisted on this, people believed otherwise for many decades.

CHAPTER 8
The Story Lives On

Year after year, people tramped through the Winchester House and marveled at its

twisting corridors and odd features. Tourists came from all over the country to see it. In 1960, a horror movie called *13 Ghosts* filmed the exterior as a setting for the creepy haunted house in the movie. Still, the Winchester House was starting to fall apart. No one was taking care of the grounds.

But in 1973, a man named Keith Kittle took

over as manager of the house. Keith, known as "Kit," had worked at Disneyland and in an Old West theme park, also in San Jose, so he knew about re-creating the past for tourists. Keith went to work. He had the Winchester House labeled a historic landmark in 1974. He put up billboards on the highway, advertising how creepy, yet historically interesting, it was. Its reputation grew.

Keith Kittle

People lined up for tours. Guides showed them the doors that opened into midair and staircases that ended at the ceilings. They could walk through the so-called séance room and the daisy

bedroom, named after the flowers in the stained glass windows.

Sometimes, the guides and other workers said they saw ghosts. One guide claims she heard a small sigh from the hallway just outside the daisy bedroom. She thought a guest must have fallen behind on the tour. But when the guide stepped into the dark hallway to find the guest, she says she saw a small dark figure take shape in front of her eyes. She stood frozen. The shape slid slowly around a corner and disappeared. Quickly, the tour guide looked around the corner. The shape was gone. Then another sigh echoed through the hall.

Had the guide just seen the ghost of Sarah Winchester herself? She believed she might have.

No one could know for sure. But this wasn't the first time workers and visitors had claimed to have seen ghosts at this historic house. In the same bedroom, a visitor had once snapped a picture. But the camera didn't seem to work well. The picture came out with a big white blob across most of the image. Just a bad camera and a coincidence? Maybe. Or maybe not . . .

A workman doing repairs several years before might have said otherwise. He was working in a part of the house called the hall of fires because it has several fireplaces. The house was quiet. No tours were going on. As he climbed halfway up a ladder, he says he felt a tap on his back. But when he turned around, no one was there. The workman shrugged off the tap. He believed that he had imagined it. He climbed the rest of the way up the ladder. Then he says he felt something again. This time, someone was *pushing* against his back. The workman whipped around. Again, no one was there. The hall was deserted and quiet.

His heart pounding, the workman climbed back down the ladder. He'd work somewhere else on the grounds that day, he decided. Something or someone didn't want him in the hall of fires.

Despite—or maybe because of—the stories of scary encounters, the Winchester House is still a tourist attraction today. People even have weddings or birthday parties there! The beautiful gardens bloom with California flowers. The woodwork is polished, and the carpets are vacuumed. To some, it looks like a lovely old mansion. But people who study ghosts and other eerie occurrences come regularly to try to capture spirits on video. In 2011 and again in 2016, the Travel Channel's show *Ghost Adventures* filmed episodes there.

The story built around Sarah Winchester has lived on. In 2018, English actor Helen Mirren starred as Sarah in a horror movie called *Winchester*.

Other Famous Haunted Houses
in the United States

The Winchester House might have strange doors and staircases, but it is not the only house in the United States with a reputation for being haunted.

The House of Death on West 10th Street in New York City is said to be haunted by many ghosts, including that of American author Mark Twain. The spirits of a young girl, a gray cat, and a woman in a white dress are also supposedly living within the walls of the House of Death.

Lizzie Borden murdered her parents with an ax in 1892 at their house in Fall River, Massachusetts. Visitors today claim that the ghosts of Lizzie's parents still walk the halls and rooms. Sometimes, they say, a ghostly face will appear on a wall of the basement.

Lizzie Borden's house

At Bell Witch Farm in Adams, Tennessee, people claim that a spirit named Kate Batts, also called the "Bell Witch," tormented a local family for years during the early 1800s. The family is long gone, but locals say the Bell Witch still haunts the farm today.

A grim history awaits visitors to the Lemp Mansion in St. Louis, Missouri, where four members of the Lemp family died by suicide in the early days of the twentieth century. Some claim their ghosts kick doors, moan, and walk around and around beds as people sleep.

At New Orleans's LaLaurie House, rumors swirled for years about the beatings and torture that Madame LaLaurie inflicted on enslaved people living in her home. Most of the stories were likely made up, but visitors still tour the mansion today, looking for the ghosts of those who died there.

A five-hundred-year-old ghost has been said to tap out messages in French on the walls of the Castle in Beaufort, South Carolina. He moves furniture around and sometimes leaves red handprints on the windows. Outside the Castle, a spirit sometimes rises from the creek, then disappears.

Parts of the movie were filmed in the Winchester House itself, and the rest was shot on a set in Australia, where the inside of the Winchester House was carefully reproduced. In the film, Sarah creeps around her dark house, draped in a black veil, haunted by the souls of the people who were killed by the Winchester rifle. This version of Sarah is quite exaggerated. And in the movie, she intends to use her house as a prison for ghosts who want revenge. The filmmakers declare that it was "inspired by true events." But is it?

Who gets to say what is true about the Winchester House and its owner? Sarah did not tell her own story. She never gave a reason for building such a large, strange house. Over the decades, neighbors, former servants, journalists, and filmmakers have all told her story for her. These *other* people have decided what is true about the Winchester House and what is not. Is it a haunted mansion filled with ghosts where a woman spoke with the spirits of the dead? Or is it a quiet woman's life's work?

No one can truly know. In the end, the only real mystery of the Winchester House is the truth.

Timeline of the Winchester House

1839 — Sarah Pardee is born in New Haven, Connecticut

1862 — Sarah marries William Wirt Winchester

1866 — Sarah and William's daughter, Annie, is born and dies five weeks later

1881 — William dies of tuberculosis

1885 — Sarah moves to California's Santa Clara Valley

1886 — Sarah buys the ranch that will become Llanada Villa

1906 — Parts of Llanada Villa are destroyed in the San Francisco earthquake

1922 — Sarah Winchester dies at the age of eighty-three

1923 — The Winchester House opens as a tourist attraction under management by John Brown

1924 — Harry Houdini visits the Winchester House

1973 — Manager Keith Kittle takes over and a major restoration of the Winchester House and grounds begins

1974 — The Winchester House is placed on the National Register of Historic Places and receives registered California Historic Landmark status

2011 — The Travel Channel films an episode of the show *Ghost Adventures* at the Winchester House

2018 — The movie *Winchester*, starring Helen Mirren, is filmed partly at Winchester House

Timeline of the World

1834 — The first group of emigrants trek successfully from Missouri to the Pacific Northwest using the Oregon Trail

1861 — The United States Civil War begins

1865 — President Abraham Lincoln is assassinated

1906 — A powerful earthquake destroys large swathes of San Francisco and areas of Northern California

1912 — The RMS *Titanic* sinks

1918 — The Spanish flu pandemic sweeps the globe, killing around fifty million people

1920 — In the United States, women gain the right to vote

1931 — "The Star-Spangled Banner" is named the United States national anthem by President Herbert Hoover

1933 — Adolf Hitler is appointed chancellor of Germany

1945 — The United States drops atomic bombs on the Japanese cities of Hiroshima and Nagasaki

1974 — President Richard Nixon resigns after the Watergate scandal

1990 — The Hubble Telescope is launched into space

2019 — The COVID-19 pandemic begins to spread around the globe

2022 — Russia invades Ukraine, causing the displacement of over fifteen million Ukrainians

Bibliography

*Books for young readers

Anderson, Cynthia. *The Winchester Mystery House*. San Jose,
    CA: The Winchester Mystery House, 1997.

Daley, Edith. *Sarah Winchester, My Neighbor*. Edited by Jim
    Fitzgerald. Orlando, FL: New Forest Books, 2018.

*Doeden, Matt. *The Winchester Mystery House: A Chilling
    Interactive Adventure*. North Mankato, MN: Capstone Press,
    2017.

Hill, Angela. "Three Ghost Stories of the Winchester Mystery
    House." *The Mercury News*, October 6, 2016. https://www.
    mercurynews.com/2016/10/06/three-ghost-stories-of-the-
    winchester-mystery-house/.

Ignoffo, Mary Jo. *Captive of the Labyrinth: Sarah L. Winchester,
    Heiress to the Rifle Fortune*. Columbia, MO: University of
    Missouri Press, 2010.

The Winchester Mystery House. San Jose, CA: The Winchester
    Mystery House, 1997.